WAY-COOL

SPANISH
Phrase Book

PASSPORT BOOKS

About this book

Jane Wightwick
had the idea

Wina Gunn
wrote the pages

Leila Gaafar (aged 10)
drew the first pictures in
each chapter

Robert Bowers
(not aged 10) drew the
other pictures, and
designed the book

Ana Bremon

did the Spanish stuff

Important things that **must** be included

First published in the United States in 2001 by

Passport Books
A division of The McGraw-Hill Companies.
4255 West Touhy Avenue, Lincolnwood (Chicago), Illinois
60712-1975 U.S.A.

Copyright© 2000 by g-and-w PUBLISHING

Printed in Singapore

Library of Congress Catalog Card Number: 0-07-138334-4

International Standard Book Number: 0-658-01691-1

03 04 05   15 14 13 12 11 10 9 8 7 6 5

CURR
PC
4121
.W47
2001

3

What's inside

Making friends

How to be cool with the group

Wanna play?

Our guide to joining in everything from hide-and-seek to the latest electronic game

Feeling hungry

Order your favorite foods or go local

Looking good

Make sure you keep up with all those essential fashions

Hanging out

At the pool, beach, or theme park—don't miss out on the action

Pocket money

Spend it here!

Grown-up talk

blah! blah! blah! blah!

If you really, really have to!

Extra stuff

All the handy things—numbers, months, dates, days of the week

my big brother
mi hermano mayor
👄 mee airmano my-yor

grandpa
abuelo
👄 abwelo

grandma
abuela
👄 abwela

dad
papá
👄 pa-pah

mom
mamá
👄 ma-mah

my little sister
mi hermana pequeña
👄 mee airmana pekenya

Half a step this way

stepfather/stepmother
padrastro/madrastra
👄 padrastro/madrastra

stepbrother/
stepsister
hermanastro/
hermanastra
👄 airmanastro/
airmanastra

half brother/half sister
medio hermano/medio hermana
👄 medyo airmano/medyo airmana

7

Hi!
¡Hola!
👄 ola

What's your name?
¿Cómo te llamas?
👄 komo tay yamas

My name's ...
Me llamo ...
👄 may yamo

Are you OK?
¿Estás bien?
👄 estas beeyen

Cool, and you?
Guay, ¿y tú?
👄 gwhy. ee too

In Spanish you put an upside-down question mark before a question, as well as one right-side-up at the end. It's the same with exclamation marks.

¿Isn't that weird? ¡You bet!

9

How old are you?

¿Cuántos años tienes?
👄 kwantos anyos tee-enes

12 years old

Doce años
👄 dosay anyos

Happy birthday!

¡Cumpleaños feliz!
👄 koomplay-anyos faileess

What's your star sign?

¿Qué signo del zodiaco eres?
👄 kay signo del sodee-ako air-res

When's your birthday?

¿Cuándo es tu cumpleaños?
👄 kwando es too koomplay-anyos

Children sing "Happy Birthday" in Spanish to the same tune. Why don't you practice:

¡Cumpleaños Feliz!
¡Cumpleaños Feliz!

Star Signs

AQUARIUS

Jan. 21 – Feb. 19
Acuario 🗨 akwaree-o

PISCES

Feb. 20 – Mar. 20
Piscis 🗨 pees-sees

ARIES

Mar. 21 – Apr. 20
Aries 🗨 a-rees

TAURUS

Apr. 21 – May 21
Tauro 🗨 towro

GEMINI

May 22 – June 21
Géminis 🗨 hemeenees

CANCER

June 22 – July 23
Cáncer 🗨 kansair

LEO
Leo image
July 24 – Aug. 23
Leo 🗨 leo

VIRGO
Virgo image
Aug. 24 – Sep. 23
Virgo 🗨 beergo

LIBRA
Libra image
Sep. 24 – Oct. 23
Libra 🗨 leebra

SCORPIO

Oct. 24 – Nov. 22
Escorpio 🗨 eskorpee-o

SAGITTARIUS
Sagittarius image
Nov. 23 – Dec. 21
Sagitario 🗨 sa-heetaree-o

CAPRICORN

Dec. 22 – Jan. 20
Capricornio 🗨 kapreecornee-o

soccer
el fútbol
⌒ el footbol

rollerskating/
rollerblading
el patinaje en línea
⌒ el patee-nahay
en leenya

music
la música
⌒ la mooseeka

electronic games
los juegos electrónicos
⌒ los hway-gos
elektroneekos

tv
la tele
⌒ la taylay

comics
los tebeos
⌒ los taybayos

teddy bears
los ositos de peluche
⌒ los oseetos
day peloochay

school
el colegio
⌒ el kolay-heeyo

spiders
las arañas
⌒ las aranyas

13

What's your ...?

¿Cuál es tu ... ?

👄 kwal es too ...

favorite group
grupo preferido
👄 groopo prefereedo

favorite color
color preferido
👄 kol-lor prefereedo

Page 51

favorite food
comida preferida
👄 komeeda prefereeda

favorite team
equipo preferido
👄 ekeepo prefereedo

favorite animal
animal preferido
👄 anee-mal prefereedo

dog
el perro
👄 el pair-ro

cat
el gato
👄 el gato

snake
la serpiente
👄 la serpee-entay

guinea pig
la cobaya
👄 la kob-eye-a

hamster
el hámster
👄 el ahmstair

parakeet
el periquito
👄 el peree-keeto

My little doggy goes *guau guau!*

A doggy (that's *"guauguau"* in baby language) doesn't say "woof, woof" in Spanish; it says *"guau, guau"* (*gwa-oo, gwa-oo*). A Spanish bird says *"pío, pío"* (*pee-o, pee-o*) and "cock-a-doodle-do" in Spanish chicken-speak is *"kikirikí"* (*kee-kee ree-kee*). But a cat does say *"miaow"* and a cow *"moo"* whether they're speaking Spanish or English!

15

Talk about school (if you can stand it)

geography
la geografía
🗣️ la heogra-feeya

art
el dibujo artístico
🗣️ el deebooho arteesteeko

PE
la gimnasia
🗣️ la heem-naseeya

Spanish
el español
🗣️ el espanyol

math
las matemáticas
🗣️ las mataymateekas

English
el inglés
🗣️ el eeng-les

music
la música
🗣️ la mooseeka

science
las ciencias
👄 las see-en-see-as

history
la historia
👄 la eestoreeya

School rules!

In Spanish-speaking countries, many children have to wear a uniform to school, and discipline is quite strict. On the other hand, they enjoy long vacation breaks: about 10 weeks in the summer and another 5–6 weeks during the school year. But before you turn green with envy, you might not like the mounds of **"tareas para las vacaciones"** (*taray-ahs para las bakasee-yones*); that's "vacation homework!" And if you fail your exams, the teachers could make you repeat the whole year with your little sister!

Gossip

Can you keep a secret?
¿Puedes guardar un secreto?
👄 pwedes gwardar oon sekreto

Do you have a boyfriend (a girlfriend)?
¿Tienes novio (novia)?
👄 tee-enes nobyo (nobya)

An OK guy/An OK girl
Un chavo bueno/Una chava buena   👄 oon chabo bwayno/ oona chaba bwayna

Way bossy!
¡Qué mandón!
👄 kay man-don (boy)
¡Qué mandona!
👄 kay man-dona (girl)

He/She's nutty!
¡Está como una cabra!
👄 esta komo oona kabra
That means "He/She's like a goat!"

"I'm not like that at all!"

What a creep!
¡Qué malasombra!
👄 kay malas-sombra

18

You won't make many friends saying this!

Bug off!
¡Vete a la porra!
betay a la porra

Shut up!
¡Cállate!
kigh-yatay

If you're fed up with someone, and you want to say something like "you silly …!" or "you stupid …!", you can start with *"pedazo de"* (which actually means "piece of …") and add anything you like. What about …

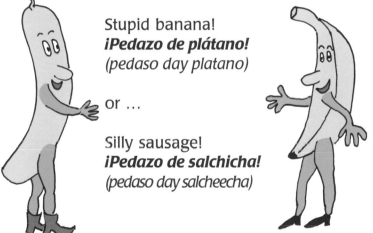

Stupid banana!
¡Pedazo de plátano!
(pedaso day platano)

or …

Silly sausage!
¡Pedazo de salchicha!
(pedaso day salcheecha)

Take your pick. It should do the trick. You could also try *"¡Pedazo de idiota!"* (pedaso day eedee-ota). You don't need a translation here, do you?

You might have to say

Fudge!
¡Ostras!
os-stras

Rats!
¡Porras!
porras

"Did someone call us?"

las ostras →

I'm fed up
¡Estoy harto! (boys)
¡Estoy harta! (girls)
estoy arto
estoy arta

That's enough!
¡Ya basta!
ya basta

I don't care
Me da igual
may da eegwal

Stop!
¡Para!
para

At last!
¡Por fin!
por feen

Saying good-bye

What's your address?
¡Cuál es tu dirección?
🗣 kwal es too deerek-syon

Here's my address
Aquí tienes mi dirección
🗣 akee tee-enes mee
    deerek-syon

Come to visit me
Ven a visitarme
🗣 ben a
    beesee-tarmay

Write to me soon
Escríbeme pronto
🗣 eskree-bemay pronto

Have a good trip!
¡Buen viaje!
🗣 bwen bee-ahay

Bye!
¡Adiós!
🗣 adeeyos

el elástico
👄 el elasteeko

el ping-pong
👄 el "ping-pong"

la pata coja
≋ la pata ko-ha

el Gameboy®
≋ el "gameboy"

los canicas
≋ las kaneekas

el yo-yó
≋ el "yo yo"

WANNA PLAY?

23

Do you want to play ...?
¿Quieres jugar ...?
👄 keyair-res hoogar

... foos-ball?
... al futbolín?
👄 al footboleen

... cards?
... a las cartas?
👄 a las kartas

... on the computer?
... con la computadora?
👄 kon la kompootadora

... tic-tac-toe?
... a las tres en raya?
👄 a las trays en righ-ya

... hide-and-seek?
... al escondite?
👄 al eskon-deetay

... catch?
... al balón?
👄 al ballon

24

Care for a game of **foal** or **donkey**?!

In Spain, you don't play "leap frog," you play "foal" —*el potro*. There is also a group version of this called "donkey"—*el burro*. This involves two teams. Team 1 lines up in a row with their heads down in the shape of a donkey. Team 2 takes turns to leap as far as they can onto the back of the "donkey." If the donkey falls over, Team 2 wins. If Team 2 touches the ground or can't leap far enough to get all the team on, then Team 1 wins—got that?! Spanish children will try to tell you this is enormous fun, but your parents might not be so happy about the bruises!

Make yourself heard

Electronic games

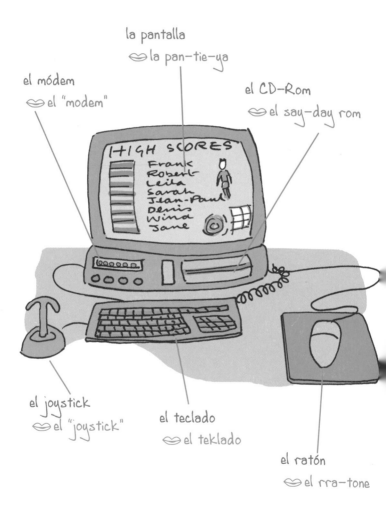

la pantalla
👄 la pan–tie–ya

el módem
👄 el "modem"

el CD–Rom
👄 el say–day rom

el joystick
👄 el "joystick"

el teclado
👄 el teklado

el ratón
👄 el rra–tone

28

What do I do?

¿Qué hay que hacer?

👄 kay eye kay asair

Show me

Enséñame

👄 ensay–nyamay

Am I dead?

¿Me han matado?

👄 may an matado

Shoot–em–up!

¡Dispárales!

👄 deespa–ralayss

How many lives do I have?

¿Cuántas vidas tengo?

👄 kwantas beedas tengo

How many levels are there?

¿Cuántos niveles hay?

👄 kwantos neebay–les eye

Non couch-potato activities!

tennis
el tenis
👄 el tenees

trampolining
el trampolín
👄 el trampoleen

bowling
los bolos
👄 los bol-los

swimming
la natación
👄 la nata-syon

hockey
el hockey
👄 el "hockey"

gymnastics
la gimnasia
👄 la heem-nasya

ballet
el ballet
👄 el ballay

basketball el baloncesto
👄 el ballon-sesto

and, of course, we haven't forgotten *"el fútbol!"*

soccer

shoes
las botas
👄 las botas

shin-pads
las espinilleras
👄 las espinee-yeras

ref
el árbitro
👄 el arbeetro

soccer gear
el equipo de fútbol
👄 el ekeepo day footbol

Good save!
¡Vaya parada!
👄 baya parada

crossbar
el larguero
👄 el largairo

goalpost
el palo
👄 el pallo

goal
el gol
👄 el gol

goalie
el portero
👄 el portairo

Pass!
¡Pasa!
👄 pasa

33

Keeping the others in line

Not like that!
¡Así no!
👄 asee no

You cheat!
¡Tramposo! (boys only)
¡Tramposa! (girls only)
👄 tramposo
   tramposa

I'm not playing anymore
Ya no juego
👄 ya no hwego

It's not fair!
¡No es justo!
👄 no es hoosto

Stop it!
¡No hagas eso!
👄 no agas eso

Showing off

Can you ...
¿Sabes ...
👄 sabays

... do a handstand?
... hacer el pino?
👄 asair el peeno

... do a cartwheel?
... dar volleretas laterales?
👄 dar boltair-retas latairal-les

Look at me!
¡Mírame!
👄 meera-may

... do this?
... hacer esto?
👄 asair esto

Impress your new friends with this!

You can show off to your new friends by practicing this tongue twister:

Tres tristes tigres comían trigo en un trigal

trays treestays teegrays comee-an treego en oon treegal

(This means "Three sad tigers ate wheat in a wheat field.")

Then see if they can do as well with this English one:

"She sells sea shells on the sea shore, but the shells she sells aren't sea shells, I'm sure."

For a rainy day

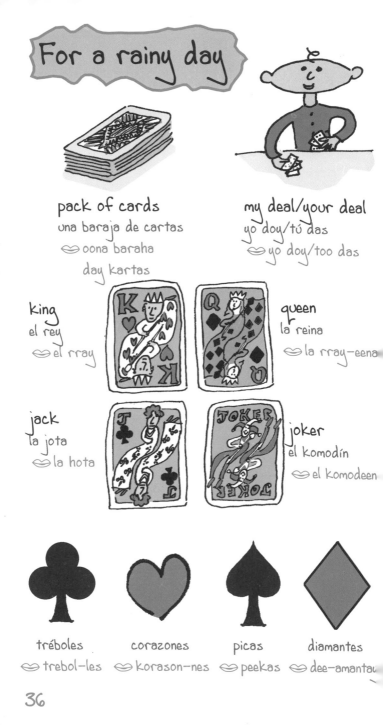

pack of cards
una baraja de cartas
☞ oona baraha
day kartas

my deal/your deal
yo doy/tú das
☞ yo doy/too das

king
el rey
☞ el rray

queen
la reina
☞ la rray-eena

jack
la jota
☞ la hota

joker
el komodín
☞ el komodeen

tréboles
☞ trebol-les

corazones
☞ korason-nes

picas
☞ peekas

diamantes
☞ dee-amantac

Do you have the ace of swords?!

You might also see children playing with a different pack of cards. There are only 48 cards instead of 52, and the suits are also different. Instead of clubs, spades, diamonds, and hearts, there are gold coins (***oros***), swords (***espadas***), cups (***copas***), and batons (***bastos***).

chessboard
el tablero
el tablairo
el alfil
el alfeel
el caballo
el kab-eye-o
el peón
el pay-on
la torre
la torray
la reina
la rray-eena
el rey
el rray

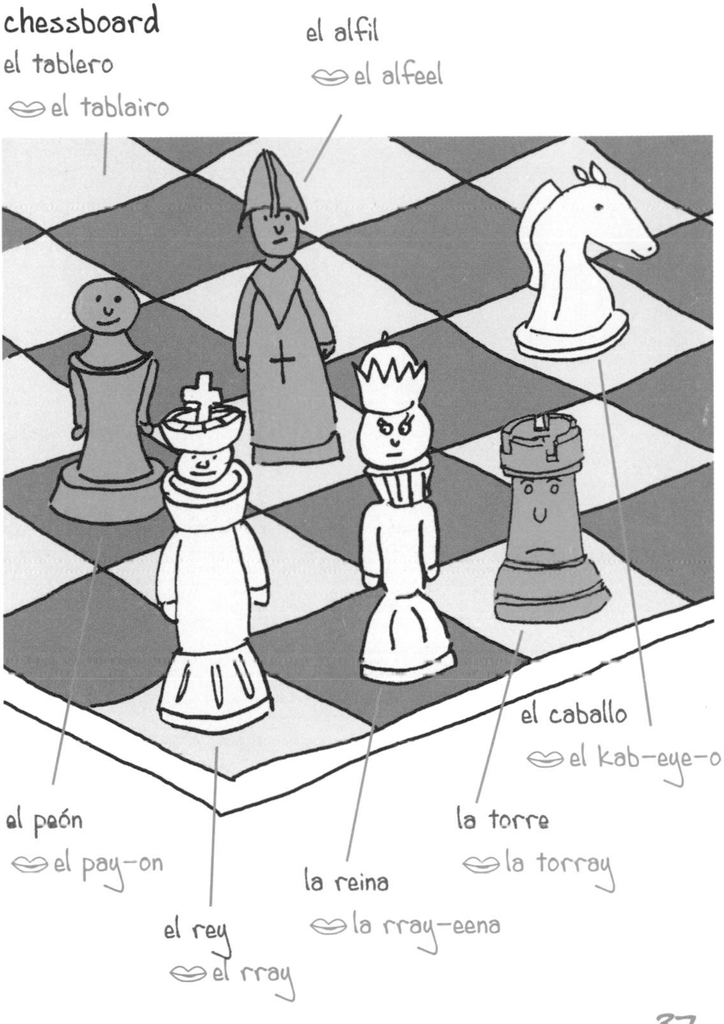

hamburger
la hamburguesa
👄 la amboorgaysa

fries
las papas fritas
👄 las papas
freetas

ice cream
el helado
👄 el elahdo

coke
una coca
👄 oona koka

F
E
E
L
I
N
G

H
U
N
G
R
Y

squid
los calamares
🔊 los kalama-res

caramel custard
el flan
🔊 el flan

la paella
🔊 la pie-eyya

orange juice
el jugo de naranja
🔊 el hoogo day naran-ha

FEELING HUNGRY

39

Grub

I'm starving
Tengo un hambre de lobo
🗪 tengo oon ambray day lobo

That means "I have the hunger of a wolf!"

Please can I have ...
Por favor, me da ...
🗪 por fabor, may da

... a cream pastry
un bollo con nata
🗪 oon boyo kon nata

... a croissant
un cruasán
🗪 oon krwasan

... a sweet roll
una palmera
🗪 oona palmayra

... a bread roll
un bollo
😮 oon boyo

... a waffle
un wafle
😮 oon wah-flay

los churros
😮 los choorros

These are wonderful sugary doughnut-like snacks. They are sold in cafés and kiosks and, in Spain, they come in a paper cone. They are also very popular for breakfast in winter, with thick hot chocolate (*chocolate con churros*).

You: Can I have some churros, Mom?

Mom: No. They'll make you fat and ruin your teeth.

You: But I think it's good to experience a foreign culture through authentic local food.

Mom: Oh, all right then.

Churros? *"¡Mm, mm!"* Garlic sandwich? *"¡Agh!"* If you're going to make food noises, you'll need to know how to do it properly in Spanish!

"Yum, yum!" is out in Spanish. You should say *"¡Mm, mm!"* And "Yuk!" is *"¡Agh!"* (pronounced "ag"), but be careful not to let adults hear you say this!

In Mexico and other countries, the *limonadas* are carbonated. So instead of a plain lemonade, you're actually getting a lemon or lime soda-pop!

... **a lemonade**

una limonada

👄 oona leemo-nadah

... **water**

agua

👄 agwa

... **a milkshake**

... un batido de leche

👄 oon bateedo day laychay

You get your hot chocolate in a large cup (to dunk your churros in).

... **a hot chocolate**

... un chocolate

👄 oon chokolatay

Did you know?

A lot of children have hot chocolate for breakfast in the morning and some of them will dip their churros or bread in it. They get very soggy and Mom is sure not to like this!

Adventures in Eating!

If you're traveling in Mexico and Central America and you don't like hot, spicy food, a good question to know is **Es picante?** (*es peekantay*—"Is it spicy?"). If the answer is no, your tongue won't catch on fire!

And if you're hungry for comfort food, you can always ask for one of the following dishes:

noodle soup

sopa de fideos
  ☞ sopa day feeday-os

spaghetti

espaguetis
  ☞ espaghetees

... with meatballs

... con albóndigas
  ☞ kon albon-deegas

you can even ask for ...

pizza

pizza
  ☞ peessa

LOOKING GOOD

nail polish
el esmalte para las uñas
✍ el esmahltay para las oonyas

headband
la diadema
✍ la dee-adema

braid
la trencita
✍ la tren-seeta

bracelets
las pulseras ✍ las poolsairas

crop top
la camiseta
✍ la kameese

belt
el cinturón
✍ el seen-tooron

miniskirt
la minifalda
✍ la minee-falda

shoes
los zapatos
✍ los sapatos

bike
la bici
✍ la beesee

46

T-shirt
la camiseta
la kameeseta

cap
la gorra
la gorra

tattoo
la calcomanía
la kalko-maneeya

jeans
los vaqueros
los bakayros

el walkman
el "walkman"

skateboard
el monopatín
el mono-pateen

tennis shoes
los deportivos
los daypor-teebos

LOOKING GOOD

47

That T-shirt please
Esa camiseta, por favor
👄 esa kameeseta, por fabor

Cool tattoo!
¡Qué calcomanía más padre!
👄 kay kalko-maneeya mass padray

The pink frilly one
La rosa con volantitos
👄 la rosa kon bolanteetos

A braid, please
Una trencita, por favor
👄 oona trenseeta, por fabor

The purple striped one
La morada de rayas
👄 la morada day righ-yas

Awesome miniskirt!
¡Vaya minifalda más chula!
👄 baya meenee-falda mass choola

Where's my skateboard?
¿Dónde está mi monopatín?
👄 donday esta mee mono-pateen

A pair of cowboys?

The word for jeans in Spanish (**los vaqueros** – *los bakayros*) actually means "cowboys" because they were the first people to wear these trousers.

48

spotted
de lunares
👄 day loona-res

flowery
de flores
👄 day flo-res

frilly
con volantitos
👄 kon bolanteetos

glittery
con brillos
👄 kon breeyos

striped
de rayas
👄 day righ-yas

jeans
los vaqueros
👄los
bakayros

T-shirt
la camiseta
👄la kameeseta

sweatshirt
la sudadera
👄la sooda-
dayra

tennis shoes
los deportivos
👄los daypor-
teebos

dress
el vestido
👄el bay-
steedo

pants
los pantalones
👄los panta-
lone-nes

skirt
la falda
👄la falda

soccer shirt
la camiseta de fútbol
👄la kameeseta
day footbol

shorts
los pantalones cortos
👄los panta-lone-nes kortos

shoes
los zapatos
👄los sapatos

50

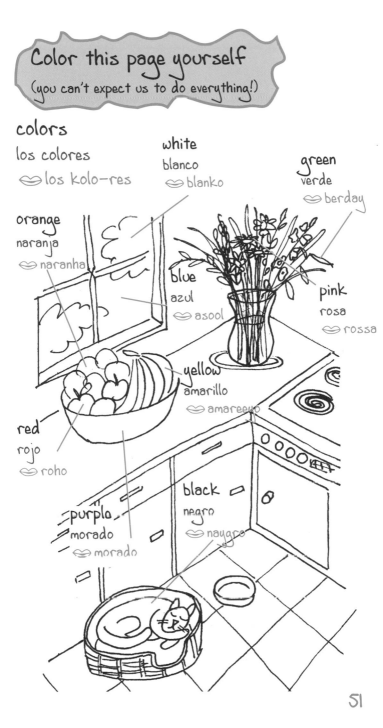

What should we do?
¿Qué hacemos?
kay asay-mos

Can I come?
¿Puedo ir?
pwedo eer

Where do you all hang out?
¿Por dónde salen ustedes?
por donday salen oos-tedays

That's mega!
¡Qué emoción!
kay aymosee-yon

I'm (not) allowed
(No) me dejan
(no) may day-han

55

sea
el mar
🗣 el mar

beach
la playa
🗣 la playa

and castle
castillo de arena
🗣 el casteeyo day arayna

towel
la toalla
🗣 la toe-aya

bathing suit
el bañador
🗣 el banyador

bucket
el cubo
🗣 el koobo

snorkel
el tubo
🗣 el toobo

shovel
la pala
🗣 la palla

shells
las conchas
🗣 las konechas

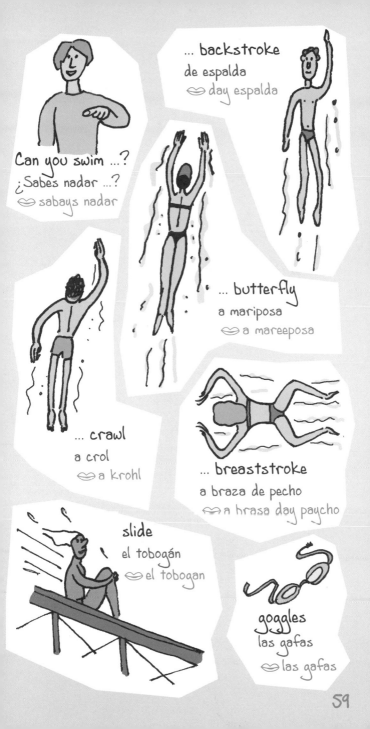

... backstroke
de espalda
day espalda

Can you swim ...?
¿Sabes nadar ...?
sabays nadar

... butterfly
a mariposa
a mareeposa

... crawl
a crol
a krohl

... breaststroke
a braza de pecho
a hrasa day paycho

slide
el tobogán
el tobogan

goggles
las gafas
las gafas

59

Downtown

Do you know the way?
¿Sabes el camino?
~ sabays el kameeno

Is it far?
¿Está lejos? ~ esta lay-hos

Are we allowed in here?
¿Nos dejan entrar aquí?
~ nos day-han entrar akee

Let's ask
Vamos a preguntar
~ bamos a pray-goontar

CLUB

ZOO

playground
el patio de recreo
≋ el pateeyo day rekrayo

slide
el tobogán
≋ el tobogan

swings
los columpios
≋ los koloom-peeyos

park
el parque
≋ el parkay

bus
el autobús
≋ el owtoboos

car
el coche
≋ el kochay

You can show off your "street smarts" to your new friends by using some slang.
A junky old car is *"una cafetera"* (*oona cafaytayra*), which means "coffee pot!" Try this: *"¡Vaya cafetera!"* (*baya cafaytayra*— "What an old clunker!").

Picnics

I hate wasps
Odio las avispas
~ odeeyo las abeespas

Move over!
¡Apártate!
~ apar-tatay

Let's sit here
¿Nos sentamos aquí?
~ nos sentamos ak

bread
el pan
~ el pan

napkin
la servilleta
~ la serbeeyeta

ham
el jamón
~ el hamon

cheese
el queso
~ el kayso

yogurt
el yogur
~ el yogur

chips
las papas fritas
~ las papas freetas

drinks
las bebidas
👄 las bebeedas

knife
el cuchillo
👄 el koocheeyo

spoon
la cuchara
👄 la koochara

fork
el tenedor
👄 el tenaydor

wasps
las avispas
👄 las abeespas

bees
las abejas
👄 las abayhas

bzzzz

ants
las hormigas
👄 las ormeegas

All the fun of the fair

slide
el tobogán
👄 el tobogan

Ferris wheel
la noria
👄 la noreeya

house of mirrors
la casa de los espejos
👄 la kasa day los espayhos

bumper cars
los coches de choque
👄 los kochays day chokay

Let's go on this
¿Nos montamos en éste?
👄 nos montamos en estay

octopus
el pulpo
👄 el poolpo

It's (too) fast
Va muy rápido
👄 ba mwee rapeedo

That's for babies
Eso es para los pequeños
👄 eso es para los pekay-nyos

Do you get wet in here?
¿En éste te mojas?
👄 en estay tay mohas

I'm not going on my own
Yo solo (boys)/sola (girls) no me monto
👄 yo solo/sola no may monto

65

Spend it here

POCKET MONEY

candy
los caramelos
⌒ los karamaylos

T-shirts
las camisetas
⌒ las kameeseta:

toys
los juguetes
⌒ los hoogaytays

el tendero
⌒ el tendayr

66

books
los libros
👄 los leebros

mobile
el móvil
👄 el mobeel

pencils
los lápices
👄 los lapeeses

POCKET MONEY

67

What does that sign say?

carnicería
butcher shop
🗫 karneesereeya

pastelería
cake shop
🗫 pastele-
reeya

panadería
bakery
🗫 panadereeya

confitería
candy store
🗫 confeete-
reeya

papelería
office supplies
🗫 papelereeya

verdulería
grocery store
🗫 berdoole-
reeya

boutique
clothes store
🗫 booteek

Money talk

Money has different names and values, depending on the country you visit.

Spain = **euros** (*ay-ooros*)
Mexico = **pesos** (*paysos*)
Guatemala = **quetzales** (*ketsalays*)
Costa Rica = **colones** (*kolonays*)

Of course, you must exchange your **dollares** (*doe-larays*) at a bank (**banco**—*banko*) or currency exchange (**casa de cambio**—*kasa day kam-beeyo*). But if you're in Puerto Rico, you're all set—the money is the same!

69

Sweet heaven!

I love this shop
Me encanta esta tienda
👄 may enkanta esta tee-enda

Let's get some candy
Vamos a comprar dulces
👄 bamos a comprar doolsays

Let's get some ice cream
Vamos por un helado
👄 bamos por oon aylado

lollipops
las piruletas
👄 las peerooletas

a bar of chocolate
una tableta de chocolate
👄 oona tableta day chokolatay

chewing gum
el chicle
👄 el cheeklay

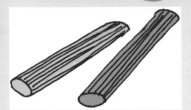

If you really want to look cool, but end up with lots of fillings, ask for:

regaliz
(regaleess)

soft licorice sticks, available in red or black

nubes (noobes)

soft marshmallow candies in different shades (**nubes** means "clouds")

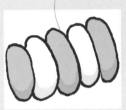

jamones
(hamon-nes)

fruity, fizzy gum in the shape of hams ("ham" is **jamón**)

Chupa-chups® (choopa-choops)

lollipops famous all over the world, but they come from Spain

polvos pica-pica (polvos peeka peeka)

tangy fizzy sherbet sold in small packets with a lollipop to dip in

kilométrico (keelomay-treeko)

chewing gum in a strip like dental floss—pretend to the adults that you're flossing your teeth!

71

Other things you could buy

(that won't ruin your teeth!)

What are you getting?
¿Qué te vas a comprar?
👄 kay tay bas a komprar

That toy, please
Ese juguete, por favor
👄 esay hoogaytay, por fabor

Two postcards, please
Dos postales, por favor
👄 dos postal-
les, por fabor

How much is that?
¿Cuánto cuesta?
👄 kwanto kwesta

This is garbage
Esto es una porquería
👄 esto es oona
porkayreeya

This rules
¡Chévere!
👄 chay–bairay

... colored pencils
... lápices de colores
🗣 lapeesays day kolo-res

I'm getting ...
Voy a comprar 🗣 boy a comprar

... felt-tip pens
... rotuladores
🗣 rotoolado-res

... a pen
... un boli
🗣 oon bolee

... stamps
... sellos
🗣 seyos

... a cassette
... una cinta
🗣 oona seenta

... a CD
... un compacto
🗣 oon compacto

... comics
... tebeos
🗣 taybayos

For many years Spain's favorite comics have been *Mortadelo y Filemón*, two accident-prone TIA agents (<u>not</u> CIA) and *Zipi y Zape*, two very naughty twins. Children also like to read *Mafalda*, an Argentinian comic, *Carlitos y Snoopy* (Charlie Brown & Snoopy), *Tintin*, *Astérix*, and *¿Dónde está Wally?* (Where's Waldo?).

75

Help!

Something has dropped/broken
Algo se ha caído/roto
algo say a kigh-eedo/roto

Please
Por favor
por fabor

Can you help me?
¿Me puedes ayudar?
may pwedes ayoodar

Where's the mailbox?
¿Dónde está el buzón?
donday esta el booson

Where are the toilets?
¿Dónde están los aseos?
donday estan los asayos

I can't manage it
No puedo
🗣 no pwedo

Could you pass me that?
¿Me pasas eso?
🗣 may pasas eso

What time is it?
¿Qué hora es?
🗣 kay ora es

Come and see
Ven a ver
🗣 ben a bair

May I look at your watch?
¿Me deja que mire su reloj?
🗣 may deha kay meeray soo reloh

77

Lost for words

... my ticket
mi billete
👄 mee beeyaytay

I've lost ...
He perdido ...
👄 eh perdeedo

... my bike
mi bici
👄 mee beesee

... my parents
mis padres
👄 mees padrays

... **my shoes**
mis zapatos

👄 mees sapatos

... **my money**
mi dinero

👄 mee deenayro

... **my sweater**
mi suéter

👄 mee swetair

... **my watch**
mi reloj

👄 mee reloh

... **my jacket**
mi chaqueta

👄 mee chakayta

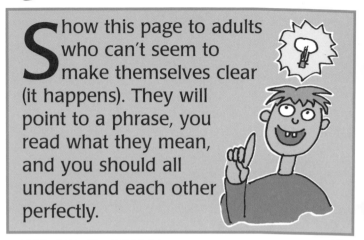

Show this page to adults who can't seem to make themselves clear (it happens). They will point to a phrase, you read what they mean, and you should all understand each other perfectly.

No te preocupes
Don't worry

Siéntate aquí
Sit down here

¿Tu nombre y apellidos?
What's your name and surname?

¿Cuántos años tienes?
How old are you?

¿De dónde eres?
Where are you from?

¿Dónde te alojas?
Where are you staying?

¿Dónde te duele?
Where does it hurt?

¿Eres alérgico a algo?
Are you allergic to anything?

Está prohibido
It's forbidden

Tiene que acompañarte un adulto
You have to have an adult with you

Voy por alguien que hable inglés
I'll get someone who speaks English

Knock, knock.

Who's there?

Uno.

Uno who?

Unos where I got this crummy joke!

uno   👄 oono

dos   👄 dos

tres   👄 trays

cuatro   👄 kwatro

cinco   👄 seenko

seis ～ sayis

siete ～ see-etay

ocho ～ ocho

nueve ～ nwebay

diez ～ deeyess

once ～ onsay

doce ～ dosay

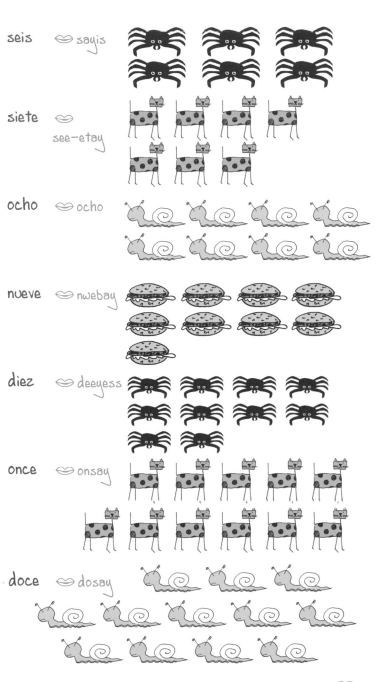

83

13	trece	*tresay*
14	catorce	*katorsay*
15	quince	*keensay*
16	dieciséis	*deeyesee sayis*
17	diecisiete	*deeyesee see-etay*
18	dieciocho	*deeyesee ocho*
19	diecinueve	*deeyesee nwebay*
20	veinte	*baintay*

If you want to say "twenty-two," "sixty-five," and so on, you can just put the two numbers together like you do in English. But don't forget to add the word for "and" (**y**, pronounced *ee*) in the middle:

32	**treinta y dos**	*traynta ee dos*
54	**cincuenta y cuatro**	*seenkwenta ee kwatro*
81	**ochenta y uno**	*ochenta ee oono*

30	treinta	*traynta*
40	cuarenta	*kwarenta*
50	cincuenta	*seenkwenta*
60	sesenta	*saysenta*
70	setenta	*saytenta*
80	ochenta	*ochenta*
90	noventa	*nobenta*
100	cien	*seeyen*

1st	primero	*preemairo*
2nd	segundo	*segoondo*
3rd	tercero	*tersayro*
4th	cuarto	*kwarto*
5th	quinto	*keento*
6th	sexto	*sexto*
7th	séptimo	*septeemo*
8th	octavo	*octabo*
9th	noveno	*nobayno*
10th	décimo	*dayseemo*

Want a date?

If you want to say a date in Spanish, you don't need to use 1st, 2nd, etc. Just say

Lunes	Martes	Miércoles	Jueves	Viernes	Sábado	Domingo
		1	2	3	4	5
6	7	8	9	10	11	12
13	14	15	16	17	18	19
20	21	22	23	24	25	26
27	28	29	30			

the ordinary number followed by **de** (*day*):

| uno de marzo | (1st of March) |
| diez de Julio | (10th of July) |

March	marzo	*marso*
April	abril	*abreel*
May	mayo	*my-yo*

June	junio	*hooneeyo*
July	julio	*hooleeyo*
August	agosto	*agosto*

September	septiembre	*septee-embray*
October	octubre	*octoobray*
November	noviembre	*nobee-embray*

December	diciembre	*deesee-embray*
January	enero	*enayro*
February	febrero	*febrayro*

primavera *preemabayra*

SPRING

verano *berano*

SUMMER

otoño *otonyo*

FALL

invierno *eenbee-erno*

WINTER

Monday	lunes	*loon-nes*
Tuesday	martes	*mar-tes*
Wednesday	miércoles	*mee-erkol-les*
Thursday	jueves	*hoo-ebes*
Friday	viernes	*bee-er-nes*
Saturday	sábado	*sabado*
Sunday	domingo	*domeengo*

By the way, many kids have a two-and-a-half hour lunch break! Time enough for lunch and a siesta. But school doesn't finish until 5 o'clock!

Good times

It's ...
Son ...
👄 sonn

(five) o'clock
las (cinco)
👄 las (seenko)

quarter after (two)
las (dos) y cuarto
👄 las (dos) ee kwarto

quarter to (four)
las (cuatro) menos cuarto
👄 las (kwatro) menos kwarto

half past (three)
las (tres) y media
👄 las (trays) ee medya

five after (ten)
las (diez) y cinco
☞ las (deeyes) ee seenko

twenty after (eleven)
las (once) y veinte
☞ las onsay ee baintay

ten to (four)
las (cuatro) menos diez
☞ las (kwatro) menos deeyes

twenty to (six)
las (seis) menos veinte
☞ las sayis menos baintay

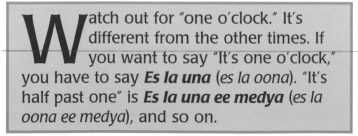

Watch out for "one o'clock." It's different from the other times. If you want to say "It's one o'clock," you have to say **Es la una** (*es la oona*). "It's half past one" is **Es la una ee medya** (*es la oona ee medya*), and so on.

91

morning
mañana
👄 la manyana

midday
mediodía
👄 el medyo-deeya

afternoon
la tarde
👄 la tarday

midnight
la medianoche
👄 la medya-nochay

evening
la noche
👄 la nochay

now
ahora
👄 a-ora

night
la noche
👄 la nochay

today
hoy
👄 oy

3 | 4 | 5 | 6
10 | 11 | 12 | 13

yesterday
ayer
👄 ayair

tomorrow
mañana
👄 manyana

93

Weather wise

Can we go out?
¿Podemos salir fuera?
👄 podaymos saleer fwera

It's hot
Hace calor
👄 asay kalor

It's cold
Hace frío
👄 asay freeyo

It's a horrible day
Hace un día horrible
👄 asay oon deeya orreeblay

It's raining seas!

In Spanish it doesn't rain "cats and dogs," it rains "seas!" That's what they say when it's raining really heavily:

¡Está lloviendo a mares! *esta yobeeyendo a ma-res*

It's windy
Hace viento
😊 asay beeyento

It's sunny
Hace sol
😊 asay sol

It's raining
Está lloviendo
😊 esta yobeeyendo

It's snowing
Está nevando
😊 esta nebando

I'm soaked
Estoy empapado (boy)/
Estoy empapada (girl)
😊 estoy empapado/empapada

It's nice
Hace buen tiempo
😊 asay bwen teeyempo

95